Resolving Conflict Peacefully

Eye Of The Hurricane

TALES OF THE
EMPTY-HANDED MASTERS

by Terrence Webster-Doyle

Atrium Society Publications
Middlebury, Vermont

Atrium Publications
P.O. Box 816
Middlebury, VT 05753

First printing 1992

Illustrations:	Rod Cameron
Cover Design:	Robert Howard
Editing and Design:	Charlene Koonce

Publisher's Cataloging in Publication Data
Prepared by Quality Books, Inc.

Webster-Doyle, Terrence.
    The eye of the hurricane : tales of the empty-handed masters /
Terrence Webster-Doyle.
      p. cm.
    SUMMARY: A series of illustrated stories and parables for young students of the martial arts, emphasizing the mental and spiritual components of their training, and the nonviolent and peaceful essence of the martial arts.

    Audience: For ages 8-15.
    ISBN 0-942941-24-1 (pbk.)
    ISBN 0-942941-25-x (cloth)
    1. Martial arts – Training – Juvenile literature. 2. Zen Buddhism and martial arts – Juvenile literature. I. Title.

GVII0l.W4 1992   796.8 QBI91-1824

Atrium publications are available at special discounts for bulk purchases, premiums, fund raising, or educational use. For details, contact:

Special Sales Director
Atrium Publications
P.O. Box 816
Middlebury, VT 05753
(800) 848-6021

Printed in Hong Kong by C & C Offset Printing Ltd.

Special thanks to Sifu Jody Sasaki and his students at the Flores Brothers Kenpo Karate Studios in Ojai, California — and to Master Joe Donnelly for helping us feel at home in Vermont.

As a mirror's polished surface reflects whatever stands before it and a quiet valley carries even small sounds, so must the student of Karate render the mind empty of selfishness in order to respond appropriately to anything that might be encountered. This is the meaning of Kara—or 'empty'—in Karate.

— Gichin Funakoshi
Father of Karate-do

To the Reader,

I've written these "Tales of the Empty-Handed Masters" to explore ideas, feelings, and aspects of training which are common to *all* Marital Arts styles. My background is mainly in Japanese Karate, and I have used certain Japanese words such as *kiai*, *hara*, *hakama*, and *gi* — certainly not out of disrespect for other styles, but simply because they are the terms I am used to. You will see that these Tales have universal significance and are meaningful to all Martial Artists, whatever their style.

Table of Contents
Tales of the Empty-Handed Masters

Dear Student,

Get ready for the greatest adventure in the Martial Arts, the adventure of getting to know yourself! In the pages that follow are tales about Empty-Handed Masters and the Art of *Kara-te* — the Art of Empty Self. The Art of Empty Self is the main intention of all Martial Arts and must be understood if one is to truly be an Empty-Handed Master.

I cannot tell you too much too soon. I will speak to you again at the end of this first series of Tales of the Empty-Handed Masters. I will only give you a hint now, a clue as to the meaning of the simple, yet profound, stories to come.

So, here is a riddle for you to think about...

What is it that...

You cannot see if you look,
You cannot hear if you listen,
You cannot take hold of if you grasp,
Is silent when you speak,
Speaks when you are silent,
And you can only have
when you don't want it?

Are you ready?
Let's find out!

The Empty Cup

One day two great and wise Martial Arts Masters were visited by a well-known and respected university professor.

"I have come a long way to see you both, since I have heard that you are great Masters of *Kara-te*, the Art of Empty Self. I have studied very hard for many years to understand the essence of what you teach. Can you tell me the meaning of *Kara-te*, of Empty Self, and how it can bring peace to the world? What is the secret of this teaching?"

The older Martial Arts Master was serving tea as the professor spoke. He poured the visitor's cup full, and still kept on pouring until the tea was running off the table onto the floor.

The professor watched the cup overflowing until she could no longer stand it. "The cup is full, no more will go in!" she exclaimed.

"Like this cup," he said, "your mind is full of questions and seeking answers! Until you empty your cup, no more can go in. Likewise, until you empty your mind, you cannot receive anything."

It is impossible to attack Emptiness or to attack from Nothingness.

Eye of the Hurricane

The night was warm. The moon had just passed behind a cloud, temporarily blocking out the light. The student could feel the hairs stand up on the back of his neck and goose bumps rise on his skin. His eyes were straining to see into the dark forest. The student felt that something or someone was waiting to attack him! As the night grew darker, the crickets became strangely quiet. His heart was pumping hard and his hands were sweating. Thoughts raced through his head. *Should I run or should I stop and fight? Where will the attack come from?*

The student came to the edge of a small clearing, a meadow that sloped down to a river. He remembered his teacher saying, "To learn about yourself is the most important thing. You will be tested constantly. You will need all your Martial Arts skills, and especially, you will need to understand the fundamental meaning of all Martial Arts: Empty Self. Understand this and you will live in the eye of the hurricane, where no one can harm you!"

The cloud moved past and the moon shone brightly, casting shadows everywhere. The student noticed two swift shadows move across the meadow to the darkness of the tall pine trees beyond. Then he heard a terrifying shout, *"KIAI!"* Then silence. There was movement among the trees, and along the border of the meadow. He was sure that something was coming towards him! His muscles became tense and he felt dizzy. The student felt the importance of this test. He was caught up in a whirlwind of thought and emotions. He wanted to charge out and challenge the attackers openly in the meadow. Simultaneously, he wanted to flee back to camp!

Be silent. Watch your thoughts; see how they jump around like a monkey. See how they cloud your mind and confuse you. He remembered these words of the Chief Instructor, offered as preparation for this test. *Your thoughts are like ripples on a still pond. You cannot act clearly when your mind is so active, running this way and that. Focus on your breathing. Count your breaths. Calm the mind and stop — look — and listen. Then focus outwardly on what's around you.*

The student closed his eyes and felt how tired they were from straining to see in the dark. His breathing was rapid and short, coming from his chest. He took a deep breath and pushed the air down into his *hara* (lower belly). One, two, three long deep breaths. He slowly counted them, while remaining alert to the sounds of the forest. The student noticed that he was more alert with his eyes closed, breathing deep into his belly. His mind slowly calmed, his muscles relaxed, and the night took on a friendly feeling. Standing alone in darkness, following his breathing, listening to the smallest sounds around him, he felt calm, still — like it must be in the eye of a hurricane. He could smell pine trees and dew on the ground. He could feel cool air on his skin. The darkness was no longer an enemy. It embraced him. The student slowly raised his bamboo sword and assumed a ready stance, quietly waiting for whatever should happen. There was no fear, no straining, no rushing thought. He opened his eyes slowly. The full moon shone brightly and equally on everything in its path. The river moved slowly without interruption, silver moonlight dancing on the water. His body was alert and ready — no thoughts of attack or defense. Just stillness, a quietness in the forest.

With arms raised above his head, the student met his attackers. Both of them emerged from the trees, with bamboo swords above their heads. Swiftly, they rushed at him from both sides. Then suddenly, they stopped... and for what seemed like forever, all three stood with their swords raised above their heads, as naturally as pine trees with branches reaching up to the light of the moon. No effort; an endless moment out of time. Then, as a leaf falls from a tree, the teachers lowered their swords and bowed towards their student. The student's sword lowered like a great wave subsiding, and he too bowed. In silence, they all knew that the test was over. There were no winners or losers. Just the forest, moon, and flowing water. They walked without talking back to the camp.

*The willow paints the wind
without using a brush.*

— Saryu

The Warrior's Bucket

It was evening as the students met in a circle near the small campfire. The hot sun was gone; the intense heat of the day had let up. The students were vividly aware of pleasant odors: pine trees, grass, flowers — even the wide river running by the camp smelled fresh and clean. They sat quietly for a few minutes, each wondering what would happen next. They had heard stories from others of being tested for skill and courage. The students were in the midst of a meadow, with trees surrounding them. The sky was dark blue with a full moon lighting the countryside in a soft white glow. One of the students was daydreaming about what was to come when she felt a sudden presence behind her and something touching her right shoulder. The student jumped and quickly turned to find a very large man with a white beard and bald head standing behind her. He had a long *shinai* (bamboo sword) in his hand, with the tip pointed towards her. The student looked up into a stern but open face. The man was dressed in a Karate *gi* (typical Karate jacket), yet he wore the traditional, more formal *hakama* (Japanese Martial Arts "skirt").

Across the other side of the circle, an older woman with dark skin and hair had appeared. She was dressed in the same outfit as the man, carrying a *shinai*, held tip down. She looked attractive and strong in her *gi* and *hakama*. The students were asked to stand and bow as these two older teachers joined them. The teachers bowed back to the students, their eyes attentive to each one of them in succession.

They all sat down. For what seemed like an hour, no one spoke. At first the students felt awkward and wanted to say something — anything! The silence was almost too much! Their minds raced with thoughts. *What are we going to do? When are we going to say or do something?*

The silence was suddenly broken by one of the teachers: "Would one of you be so kind as to fill this bucket half full of water from the river?" He held out a wooden bucket. Without thinking, the student stood up and said, "I will!" She walked over to the older man. He smiled and handed her the bucket.

"Good, young lady. You are very eager." The student walked rapidly down to the river, feeling the eyes of the whole group upon her. *Why did I volunteer?* she thought. She felt she had to break that silence; she'd do anything just to talk again! She knelt down at the river's edge and placed the bucket into the water, almost losing it in the rushing water. The water filled the bucket quickly, overflowing its brim. It was so heavy that she strained to pull it back out of the river. She tipped the bucket and let half of the water fall back into the river. Then she walked lopsidedly, with the bucket splashing out water, back to where the group was waiting, the bright moon lighting her way.

What does he want with this water? Are we going to drink it? Or is this one of the 'tests' I've heard about? The student's brain rushed with thoughts. She placed the bucket in front of the two teachers. The older man motioned to the older woman and she shook her head *no,* then gestured approval to him. He looked at the students, especially at the student who had brought the water from the river, and slowly began rolling up the right sleeve of his *gi*. All the students were wondering what was happening. Then the teacher raised his arm above the bucket and slowly let his arm drop down toward the bucket

14

until his hand disappeared inside it. He began to stir the water around, splashing some of it out on the ground, smiling as he did so. The student could stand it no longer. "Sir, excuse me for asking, but why are you doing that?"

"For the joy of it! Because it feels good!" he replied seriously... then he laughed. The student's mind suddenly stopped thinking, as if it had hit a brick wall! *What?* was the only question that rang in her brain.

"Young lady, you cannot get here from there," he said. He then took his arm out of the water, stood up and walked away into the woods.

My storehouse having been burnt down,
Nothing blocks the view
of the bright moon.

— Masahide

Time Stands Still

The students' training at camp consisted of daily meditation, duties, physical training, and "mental freestyle" (as they called it). "Mental freestyle" was a time set aside to sharpen mental alertness and understanding; the students would soon find out that this was the most important part of the training. There was also a time set aside for special activities involving the application of important principles of the Martial Arts.

The students were awakened each morning by a bell. The first morning the boy heard it through his sleep. A solid metal strike, then a strong sound spreading out like ripples on a lake. One, two, three — the echo in the mountains — one, two, three. This series of gongs was repeated three times. It was not a harsh sound, yet it was strong enough to reach into his sleep; it entered his dreams to bring him to wakefulness on the wings of vibration. He listened to the echo and the pure metallic sound. For a moment there was *only* that sound — no one listening. It was such a peaceful moment, but then the boy began to wonder what the day would bring.

They met at the river. Standing in the early morning sun, looking up at the mist-covered mountains, he felt so happy — as if he were a small child within a secure home. "Home at last, home at last," he repeated softly to himself. *What a relief!* A heron stood in the river, silently, without motion — behind it, a background of pine-forest green. The heron seemed so naturally a part of the woods and river. He could not see one without the other. A tranquil scene.

The boy suddenly leapt into the mountain stream, letting out a yell. They had been instructed to bathe in silence, but the water was so cold that the scream escaped spontaneously. It was as if a frozen knife had stabbed him; then he felt wide awake! The heron didn't move at all, as if it felt that what the students were doing was perfectly natural.

After this first early morning swim, they dried off and put on their *gis*. The boy enjoyed walking in his *gi* on the stone path, feeling so clean and refreshed. The wonderful odor of honeysuckle filled the air; he leaned over to smell a flower. As he had been lost in the bell's sound, so he was lost in that odor of honeysuckle. For a brief yet everlasting moment, he was gone. He couldn't explain how or why or what it felt like — but he was just not there. There was only the honeysuckle, the sweet odor of the flower — that's all.

The long night.
The sound of water
Says what I think.

— Gochiku

The Hungry Tigers

Sitting in the cool shade of the forest under magnificent giant pine trees, the group of students gathered to hear their chief instructors tell their tales:

"There was a man traveling across a field who encountered a tiger. The man fled, the tiger chasing after him. Coming to a cliff, the man caught hold of a vine and swung himself down over the edge. The tiger sniffed hungrily down at him. Trembling, the man looked down to where, far below, another hungry-looking tiger was staring up at him. Only the vine held him from both these beasts.

"Then suddenly from nowhere, two mice appeared and began gnawing away at the vine. With a hungry tiger above and one below, and the mice gnawing away at his life line, the man suddenly noticed a delicious ripe strawberry growing on the side of the cliff. Holding on to the vine with one hand, he picked the strawberry with the other. How sweet it tasted!"

One of the instructors said to the students, "These tales all point to what cannot be pointed to: Empty Self."

Every time the students wanted to know about the true meaning of the Martial Arts — Empty Self — they received strange answers or even questions. For example, one of the students asked, "Teacher, what is the meaning of the Martial Arts? Where does Empty Self come from?" To which the instructor replied, "Where does this question of yours come from?"

The geese fly back to country after country without a calendar.

— Shumpa

The Test of the Wild Horse

"Students, today you will be tested by a wild horse." The chief instructor directed her three senior students to a narrow ravine where a wild horse grazed. She instructed them to go through the ravine and meet her on the other side where she would wait for them.

The first student stood and started through cautiously. Part way in, the wild horse charged him, flailing his hooves. The student skillfully blocked and dodged the hooves and made it through to the other side.

The next student stood at the entrance, deep in thought. Instead of entering the ravine directly, he decided to climb up the sides of the ravine and pass above the horse. The horse tried to charge the student, but the student was too high up. He successfully passed the wild horse and reached the other side.

The third and last student stood at the entrance of the ravine. Both students and the instructor at the other end waited and watched. The third student sat down on the ground and started to play as if she were a child. The wild horse, curious, came up to the student who was playing with sticks in the dirt. Calmly and gently, the student reached out and stroked the horse's nose and slowly stood up and patted its neck and mane. The horse, sensing the student's calmness and kindness, stood still as the student got up on its back. Together they rode through the ravine to where the other students and their teacher were waiting.

The morning glory blooms but an hour
And yet it differs not at heart
From the giant pine
that lives for a thousand years.

— Matsunaga Teitiku

The Miracle of the Martial Arts

When the students reached town, they went immediately to the local school of Martial Arts for the special demonstration. People had come from far and wide to discover what they had been told was "the secret of the Martial Arts," the real miracle that this practice offered. This town's school had invited a famous Martial Arts teacher from far away to demonstrate this mysterious secret.

Students and instructors gathered in groups, all dressed in different Martial Arts outfits representing all styles and many schools of the Martial Arts. The air was alive with excitement. The people were asked to be silent.

The guest instructor entered, dressed in a simple Karate *gi* tied with a frayed Black Belt and sat down on a cushion in the very center of the room. He looked old but strong.

For a long while, he sat quietly. Then, breaking the silence, a young student called out: "Are you such a great Master that you know the real secret of the Martial Arts? You don't look like anyone special!" said the young man brashly. "My Master," he continued, "is the greatest Master of all time. He can defeat ten men with one hand tied behind his back. He can even break bones with his bare hands. Can you do such miracles of strength, old man?" the young man challenged.

The visiting teacher smiled at the impudence of the young student and replied lightly, "Perhaps your teacher can perform such miraculous tricks, but I have no use for them." The student looked puzzled. "That is not the way of my Martial Art. My miracle is that when I feel hungry, I eat and when I feel thirsty, I drink."

The poppy flowers;
How calmly
They fall.

— Etsujin

Heaven in a Wild Flower

They had traveled to the country, away from the camp. Their teacher had invited three apprentices to go on a nature walk, as they had often done before. To be in nature was an important part of their training. The day was warm and sunny, the air fresh with the newness of early summer. They walked quietly through the fields so as not to disturb the wildlife.

The teacher knelt down on the ground in the midst of a patch of pure white wild flowers. On closer inspection, one could see a beautiful purple pattern inside each one. These flowers were usually alone in their splendor, with no one to compliment them on their beauty. The teacher brought out a magnifying glass and held it over one of the flowers. He motioned to his students to look closer into the flower. Deep inside, on a drop of dew, was a tiny black and yellow spider suspended on the thin surface of a water droplet.

"Oh, students, what wonder, here in this patch of wild flowers!" the teacher exclaimed. "This is the essence of beauty, the meaning of *Kara-te do* — Empty Self!" One felt a sense of timelessness while staring down at that small flower and its tiny inhabitant on the dewdrop. The mind was quiet.

Soon they came upon the forest's edge on the ridge of a hill and walked quietly among pine trees. The movement of the wind through the trees sounded like waves in the ocean.

"Oh, students, can you hear that? Do you hear the pine waves? Nature speaks to us. This too is the essence of Empty Self, the essence of the Martial Arts." The teacher spoke softly and with affection.

As day turned into evening, the small group walked back from the country. That night the apprentices were to meet their other teacher, and they felt especially alert, for they knew they would be tested again. Lights were coming on as they entered the camp. When they reached the main training hall, the apprentices were told to wait outside until summoned.

The first student was called in. As she began to enter, she noticed a wooden bowl balanced delicately over the curtained entrance to the room. If she opened the curtain, the bowl would have fallen on her. Seeing this, she took it down, entered the room, and replaced the wooden bowl back over the entrance.

The second student was called in. He pulled back the curtains and the bowl fell, but he caught it and placed it back where it had been.

When the third, and youngest, student was called in, he rushed through the curtains and the wooden bowl fell. "Ouch!" he exclaimed as he rubbed his head.

"You are too careless, young student, and for this you must wash all the dishes for the week's meals. Next time you will be more aware."

The young student bowed to his teachers and fellow apprentices. "Thank you for teaching me about *Kara-te*. I have learned not only from the beauty of a wild flower and pine waves, but also from an ordinary wooden bowl! My training now teaches me to wash dishes with humility."

*The wild geese do not intend
to cast their reflection.
The water has no mind
to receive their image.*

— Zenrin Kushu

The Lesson of Nothingness

The young student had been studying the Art of *Kara-te* for six years. She started when she was seven and she was now thirteen. During those six years she had diligently practiced the physical forms, excelling in this part of her study. One day she was called into her teacher's private meeting room. The student wondered why the teacher had summoned her. Perhaps she would be promoted to a higher rank.

The teacher sat quietly for a moment with the student. "Young lady," the teacher spoke with respect, "you have been an excellent student. You have learned the forms well. But this is only a very small part of the Art of *Kara-te*. Today I want to show you the essence of this wonderful art."

On the table between the young student and her teacher was a ripe red apple.

"Here is an apple, take it."

"Yes, teacher," replied the girl.

"Break it open."

"It is broken, teacher."

"What do you see there?"

"Some small seeds, teacher."

"Break one of these."

"It is broken, teacher."

"What do you see there?"

"Nothing at all."

The teacher said, "Student, that nothingness which you do not see is the very essence of the apple tree. That nothingness is also the essence of all things, even you, young student, for all things come from it and go back to it."

"Tell me more, teacher," said the student.

The teacher gave the student a small bag of salt, saying, "Place this salt in a glass of water and come to me tomorrow with the glass."

When the student came back the next day, the teacher said, "Bring me the salt which you put in the water."

The student brought the glass of water to the teacher, saying, "The salt has disappeared."

"Taste the water from the lip of the glass and tell me how it is."

"Salty," said the student.

"And from the middle?"

"Salty."

"And from the bottom?"

"Salty also."

The teacher said, "Like this salt in the water, everything fills everything; all is in all and you are that."

The young student bowed to her teacher and left silently.

Sitting quietly, doing nothing,
Spring comes, and the grass
grows by itself.

— Zenrin Kushu

The Empty Boat

It was dawn and the birds were singing morning songs. The faint mist on the lake was rising and the sun was beginning to shine through. A beaver's lodge, one of the dwellings of the forest, stood out where a small river fed the lake. An occasional fish jumped out of the water, breaking the mirrored surface, sending ripples outward until they disappeared into stillness again. A red-tailed hawk soared overhead and the cool air felt soothing.

"Suppose you are in a boat crossing this lake," said the teacher gently, barely breaking the silence, "and another boat, an empty one, comes out of nowhere and is about to collide with your boat. Would you lose your temper on seeing this empty boat, or would you simply change the course of your boat so as to avoid the collision? But suppose there was someone in that other boat. Would you shout at that person to watch out? And if that person did not respond, as you called out again and again, would you yell still louder and even threaten that person? With the empty boat there was no anger, but when the boat was occupied there was ill feeling. Can you, oh students, go through life as if coming upon an empty boat?"

The mist was rising and the hawk cried out. There was a feeling of great joy, as if the sky and earth were endless. The heart opened and the brain was quiet.

"Teacher, how do I understand *Kara-te*, the art of Empty Self? Where do I start?" a student spoke up.

"Do you hear the sound of that hawk's cry?"

"Yes, I do."

"Start from there."

Far in the distance, nestled against the green mountains, a small cottage could be seen. The breeze had picked up and moved the mist from the lake. A single robin chirped its morning call. Bright yellow dandelions dotted the fresh, wet green fields. The order of nature seemed timeless and the green mountains sloped softly, gently carving out the space between earth and sky. A curious ant crawled over the foot of the teacher.

"Teacher, what is death?"

"Who dies?" replied the teacher.

"But I am afraid to die," said the student.

"Tell me, student, what you think death is."

"It is a black hole, a dark room, a big door closing, the end of everything."

The teacher closed his eyes as if he were resting. "How do you know what you say is true?" he spoke gently upon opening his eyes.

"I have been told this by others, Teacher."

"Is that death? Isn't death the unknown? What you tell me of death is the known, what others have told you it is. And now this is what you know. So what is death?"

On hearing this, the student bowed.

The sun was moving up the sky as the students began to practice their forms.

Upon the clatter of a broken tile
All I had learned
Was at once forgotten.

— Anonymous

Everyday *Kara-te*

The students were gathered in the hall for their evening talk. They had been practicing their forms all day and were quite tired, but they were looking forward to this time. They would talk with their teachers about the meaning of *Kara-te* and how this practice could be applied in their everyday lives.

The hall became quiet when the teachers arrived. The teachers sat with the students and nodded their greetings. Outside, the wind was blowing hard and the branches of pine trees scraped against the building. Clouds moved quickly across the dark sky, frequently blocking out the light of the moon. A storm was approaching.

"Teachers," said one of the new students, "I have come from far away to study the Art of *Kara-te* with you. Will you please teach me?"

"Have you eaten yet?" replied one of the teachers.

"Yes, teacher, I have just finished."

"Good," said the teacher. "Then go wash your bowl."

Life is after all
Like the butterfly
However that may be.

— Soin

Winning by Losing

That night it thundered terribly. The school shook with each roar. Then a great flash! The sky lit up as if it were day. One, two, three streaks at a time, the lightning stretched across the sky from heaven to earth. The rain beat down in buckets on the roof. The students pressed their faces against the windows, feeling excitement, fear and awe.

Earlier in the evening the students had practiced their forms against the heavy rain and strong winds. Time and again they fell into the mud, their *gis* turning chocolate brown. Block, punch, kick — over and over they practiced, using the rain and wind as their opponents. The rain hit hard on their bodies and soaked through their *gis*. They fought the weather until they were exhausted.

"Again, students," the teacher shouted above the wind and rain. "Fight the wind, fight the rain!" The students continued to fight against the storm. "Now turn and let the storm be at your backs. Go with it! Don't resist! Use nature's force as your own." The students turned and let the wind hit them from behind. They continued to practice their forms until they felt the exhaustion pass and their spirits lift. Then it was as if the wind and rain began practicing with them, the stormy weather becoming their ally. The students had stopped resisting and, in so doing, they had conquered themselves and learned to dance with the elements. They now understood the term, "winning by losing."

When walking, just walk
When sitting, just sit
Above all, don't wobble.

— Old Saying

The Razor's Edge

"Students, you train as if you are dancing alone, striking at ghosts in the air! This is not real *Kara-te*. You need to feel the challenge of attack to be empty, to be still and alert. This alertness, this stillness of attention, is the main reason for learning this Art. Without it, you would be walking as if in a dream. Most people spend their lives sleepwalking, not noticing what is around them, mainly concerned with themselves and their pleasures," emphasized the teacher.

This would be the morning of the students' greatest adventure. The day was hot and still. The sun reflected brightly off the lake's water and the bugs were out in swarms. The grass underfoot felt brittle and dry.

"From today on, until we say it is enough, you will be under attack. When you least expect it, we will be there to hit you with our bamboo swords. Do you understand?"

"Yes, teachers," the students replied hesitantly.

The students went about their daily practice and chores nervously, readying themselves for the attack. There was an air of tension in the camp. Morning came and went. The afternoon got hotter. Even the birds stopped singing; the animals rested in cool spots deep in the forest. The afternoon gave way to twilight, but still nothing remarkable had happened.

"Was it just a joke?" one student asked another at dinner time.

"Maybe they were just trying to frighten us," the other student answered.

As these two were washing dishes after dinner, they sensed a sudden presence behind them. Too late to turn! They felt a sharp whack on their shoulders. Before they could recover, the door closed behind them, leaving the room empty but for the two students rubbing their shoulders. They were stunned but not really hurt.

As the students lay in bed that night, they heard a slight creaking sound. Then suddenly, in the dark, there were shouts. "Ouch!" "Yeow!" "Ouch!" voices exclaimed in surprise and shock. Someone ran for the lights and when they were on, six students could be seen moving around the sleeping area rubbing their backsides.

"Oh, that stings!" one exclaimed. "Ouch, that hurts," another complained. They all looked around for the culprits, but no one could be found. The door out of the room was swinging slightly.

These attacks went on for days. Night after night, the attacks went on. After a week, the students decided they had endured enough. They agreed to pretend to be asleep that night so they would be prepared for their attackers.

Just after midnight, they heard the creaking sound of someone walking across the wooden floor.

"*KIAI!*," they shouted as they jumped up fully clothed in their *gis*. Someone had been stationed by the lights and turned them on just at that moment.

"Good evening, students. We thought you would like some tea and cookies after your long and weary battles," said one of the teachers, carrying a tray of cookies and a large pot of tea.

They all had a good laugh and sat down together and enjoyed their late night meal.

The attacks continued over the next few days and nights, but now the students met the attackers (their teachers) with

proper blocks to fend off the bamboo swords. They became so good at this that they could defend against any attack the teachers would bring upon them.

"Now, students, you are living Empty Self. You have awakened from your dream state and live on the razor's edge of attention. But I must warn you," said the teacher cautiously, "watch out! There is someone behind you!"

All the rains of June
and one evening, secretly,
through the pines, the moon.

— Ryota

Instant Black Belt

A hummingbird was caught in the screened porch of the school building. It darted madly about, hitting the screen, its wings a blur of activity, trying to escape its prison.

"Oh, little bird, there is nothing to fear," said the teacher gently as he walked out onto the porch. "Be calm, no one is going to hurt you. Just stop for a moment so I can help you."

The teacher started humming a gentle song as he moved towards the hummingbird. The bird had come to rest on a hanging plant. The teacher walked slowly up to the plant and grasped the bird ever so tenderly. He could feel the tiny bird's tremendous energy in his hand, a vibrant being which, for the moment, seemed to trust its temporary captor. This was intensely focused life force... extraordinary!

He walked with the hummingbird over to the screen door and opened it with his free hand. Slowly he raised his other hand, which held the bird, and relaxed his fragile grasp. The hummingbird rested for a moment in the teacher's hand, then suddenly flew away with amazing speed, darting this way and that through the flower garden by the school and out to the open meadow, in a blur of energy.

The teacher waved good-bye to the bird and came back inside to where the students were sitting. "Today, students, who would like to become an instant Black Belt?"

All around the room hands went up, waving wildly in anticipation of such a desired goal — that magical, powerful symbol that all Martial Artists work so hard for.

"Come here, young man," the teacher motioned to a young boy sitting in front. He took a belt from a bag next to him and

put it on the student. "Today you are Black Belt for a day. Let's practice now," the teacher directed.

The assistant instructors lined the students up, including the new Black Belt. For the next hour, they practiced vigorously, especially the young man wearing his new symbol of power. After practice, the teacher asked them all to sit down once again.

"So how did it feel, young man?" he asked, looking over at him.

"I felt powerful! I felt as if I could fight ten grown men!" he replied energetically.

"So where did you get all this power from?"

"From this Black Belt," he replied proudly.

The teacher stood up and took off his Black Belt and held it up. He said, "What do you see, students?"

Hands raised quickly in response to his question. "Power!" "Strength!" "Wisdom!" "Energy!" they called out.

One student way in the back said, "Teacher, I only see a black piece of cloth."

"So where does this great power come from if this is only a black piece of cloth?" he questioned the student in the back.

"From our minds, from the images that we have of that piece of cloth."

"And is that real power, real strength, real wisdom?" asked the teacher.

The students were quiet for a moment before one of them answered, "No teacher, that power is empty, that wisdom is false. There is no strength in a piece of black cloth."

"Then what is the purpose of a belt?" the teacher asked.

"To hold up your pants," one of the students exclaimed.

They all laughed and laughed, until there were tears in their eyes.

A lovely thing to see:
Through the paper window's hole,
the Galaxy.

— Issa

The Simple Lesson of Water

The students were called together into the main hall. "Today, students, you will learn a simple yet profound lesson. It is an easy one that even a small child can do," the Master teacher said. "I want you to find a partner, or I'll appoint one for you." Some of the students ran to their friends, while some, looking shy, milled around, not really looking for anyone. Finally all the students were paired off.

"Now, each pair choose a blindfold. One of you will be blindfolded," said the teacher, "and the other will be the leader." One student in each pair was then blindfolded. "I have designed a course for you leaders to take your blindfolded partners through. Can you see the different markers that have just been placed around the room?" The leaders looked around the large room at the marked course.

"The game is very simple. Guided by your leader, you will feel whatever your leader guides you to. Don't worry, we have no harmful things for you to touch. Everything is safe. Well, there might be a scary thing or two!" Some of the students shivered at the thought of what they might have to touch.

Slowly, the blindfolded students were led around the large hall, each one touching whatever their leader asked them to touch. Occasionally a scream would break the silence, when one of the students touched an object that was scary, or a surprise to him or her. This made the lesson all the more fun.

There were all sorts of things to experience through touch — rough things, smooth things, squishy things, slippery things, hard and soft things. At the end of the course there was a large bowl of water. Every student who put his or her hand into that water jumped in surprise. At the end of the blindfolded course, the students took off their masks.

"Now students, those of you who just went through the course blindfolded will go through again without the blindfold. This time, both feel the object and look at it."

The students did what they were told and, at the end of the course, they again came to the large bowl of water. Each student put a hand into the water. This time no one jumped in surprise.

"Let's sit down," the teacher requested. The teacher joined the group, sitting cross-legged on the floor. "Now tell me what you experienced." Many descriptions were given — some pleasant, some not.

"How did you feel when you first touched the water with your blindfold on?" the teacher asked.

All the students replied that they were startled by the water, that they jumped when they touched it.

"Was the water so cold or hot that it made you jump?" the teacher enquired.

"No," replied a student. "It was just a surprise. We didn't know that it was water."

"And the second time around, without the blindfold — did you jump then when you touched the water?" the teacher enquired.

"No," the student replied.

"Why not?" asked the teacher.

"Because I recognized that it was only water. I saw it before I felt it, so it didn't surprise me like it did the first time. The first time I couldn't see it, so I didn't know what it was. The second time I could see what it was, and I knew what to expect," he replied.

"What can you learn from this lesson that is very simple yet of great importance, not only to your life but to world peace?" the teacher asked seriously.

The students were puzzled by this question. *What is the connection between touching water and world peace?* they thought to themselves.

"I don't understand what you mean," the same student replied. "The only difference I see in the two instances is that the first time we had no knowledge of the water and did not expect it, so we were surprised. It was like touching something for the first time, like when I was very young and played at the edge of the ocean. It was a new experience. The second time we all knew that the bowl contained water and knew what to expect. Therefore, we were not surprised."

"So, you had no knowledge, no expectation, at first and therefore you experienced water as if it were new to you. That was a very different feeling from the second time when you *knew* that it was water, and the experience was just ordinary. Can you see the different state of mind present in these two experiences?" the teacher asked.

"Now suppose you think about this lesson and how it applies to your daily life. How often are things new — extraordinary — to you, like when you were a small child? And how much do we 'know' about life — in a way that makes things, people and places old, familiar, rather dead? Can you see the importance of approaching life freshly, without the burden of knowledge from the past?

"Now, let's take a big leap and apply this experience you've just had to thinking about yourselves in relationship. If your mind hangs on to old memories, especially ones of hurt

and fear, and carries those experiences over into new relationships, what happens? Your mind is not fresh, new. It is burdened with past memories and is disturbed, troubled. This carrying over of a problem from the past creates problems now. If one's mind is not peaceful, then the world is not peaceful; for our thoughts create our actions and our actions create the world. If the mind is old, dead, caught in the past, what does the real miracle of ordinary life become? Can we experience life like a small child, and really feel the joy of looking afresh each moment? This, dear students, is at the heart of the Martial Arts. For to have an empty mind, a mind that is not filled with past hopes, fears, hurts, prejudices and hates, is to have a mind that is free, peaceful and truly loving. Think deeply about this, for it is the greatest lesson!

"Our activity today was a simple example of how the mind, by living in the past, takes the newness out of life. See how the mind does this in other ways, how it stores a collection of memories that becomes 'you' and 'me,' 'us' and 'them' — each with our beliefs about life based on those memories. See how this creates conflict by separating us, one from the other.

"Observe your minds and watch how this occurs, how the brain stores these memories, especially of being hurt emotionally. From past recollections, 'I know that I have been hurt and know I have to protect myself.' And collectively, 'We have been hurt and know we must protect ourselves.' See the danger of this, how this creates war within and without! Oh, students, this may be difficult for you to fully comprehend, but it is so very important! You are not expected to understand all of this now. What you are being asked to do is to begin to observe your mind, the mind that is the mind of all people, and to see how certain memories cause conflict in relationship. Just begin with simple observations, as with the bowl of water, and move from there. You will, in so doing, discover the root of human violence and conflict, for it is within ourselves. We create the world; we are the world. When our minds are filled with fear, hurt, anger and hate, then we create that in the world. Can we 'empty' the mind of all this unnecessary knowledge? Then we will really be living the art of Empty Self. Think deeply about this, for it is the greatest lesson!"

The students and teacher bowed as an end to their class.

With freshly-pulled carrot
The farmer points the way.

— Issa

One Encounter — One Chance

The students had been working in the school's garden all morning. The dirt was a dark brown and felt soft and cool under their bare feet. One of the students, on her knees and digging with her hands in the soil, exclaimed, "Oh, look at this one!" as she held up a large brown potato with a smaller one clinging to it.

They grew all their own food, except for wheat and rice, which they bought in town. Fresh cabbages, carrots, beets, lettuces, peas, and lots of squash. Growing their own food organically was different from their experiences with food at home. Out in nature, food tasted so different — so fresh and healthy. Everyone took turns planting and tending the garden, as well as cooking and cleaning. These were all natural parts of everyday living together. It was also a natural part of their Martial Arts practice.

The school had two cats. They lived a lazy life. The students would find them curled up sleeping in the oddest places — like in the old tool shed, in one of the students' lockers, or on a window ledge in the morning sun. But one of their favorite places was on the practice hall porch. As the students practiced their forms, the cats would stretch, yawn, and curl up, or dangle half off a ledge.

"Do you see how relaxed those cats are?" the teacher asked the students one day in the practice hall. "That is the relaxation needed to practice your forms well. When you are tense, you cannot move correctly. Your mind and body are stiff from trying too hard to succeed. You think of winning or losing, you become hard and tight, and there is no beauty in your

movements. Practice the beauty of your forms. Forget about winning or losing. There is no beginning or end to your practice. The first movement is the last movement. Do you understand?"

Then he picked up a towel laying nearby. "You see how I snap the towel like this?" he asked. "Can you hear the sharp crack as I flick it so? The towel is relaxed before and is relaxed just after the point of contact. Only at the point of contact, or extension, does it tense and become focused. Your techniques should be like that. For just a brief moment, tense, focused — then relax, relax, relax."

The students continued practicing their forms as the teacher snapped the towel. And the cats rolled over into new sleeping positions, as if they had been poured there.

"Students, you try too hard but not hard enough. Do you understand?"

"No, Sir, I don't," said one of the junior students. "You tell us to relax, not try too hard. Then you tell us that we are not practicing hard enough! I am confused by what you say."

"You are not letting go. You hold back; you are resisting really punching. No one will get hurt if you observe the limitations I have set for you. Since you are not allowed to make contact, this should free you to give yourself up fully to each technique. You must go beyond yourself. Perhaps you do not understand all that I say, but don't worry. Just listen, no matter how little you seem to understand or not understand. Like fertile ground, seeds will grow. Just keep open like a field ready to be sown."

The teacher counted punches as the students punched harder and harder. "Now try harder, harder!" he commanded. "One hundred punches, two hundred punches!" The students sweated pools of water as they punched and punched — and punched!

"Now stop," he said loudly! "Jump up and down, shake everything loose. Now get back into your fighting positions again. We will do ten 'One Encounter — One Chance' punches. Each punch must be as if it is your last. You have only *one* chance! Calm your breathing, calm your mind, relax your body, but remain attentive. Just listen to me — don't look my way. Now, are you ready?"

There was silence in the room. The cats had woken up and were intently staring at the students; the cats too were relaxed but ready.

"One!"

"*KIAI!*" The combined shout of the students shook the school.

"Two!"

"*KIAI!*" And again the walls shook.

"Three!" "Four!" "Five!"

In unison, the students *kiaied* with greater and greater intensity, as if rising to some great height.

"Six!" "Seven!" "Eight!" "Nine!"

Stronger and stronger they punched; louder and louder they *kiaied*.

"Now, this is your last and only chance. You must let go completely of any resistance you have. You must break through that wall holding you back. You must go beyond yourself!"

"Ten!" he shouted.

"*KIAI!*" The students responded in perfect unison.

When the noise of the *kiais* subsided, the practice room was vibrating with energy. Everyone was wide awake. The towel had been snapped and the great power unleashed. This power was not the power of violence. It was passion, pure natural energy, like lightning or thunder. Everyone stood quietly in the awe of that moment. The sun shone brightly through the window where the cats had been.

To subdue the enemy without fighting is the highest skill.

— Gichin Funakoshi

Who Is the Enemy?

As they walked silently in the forest, the students came upon a grove of birch trees, white with peeling bark. A blue jay darted out and flew quickly for cover in the lush trees beyond. The school dog ran ahead of them, stopping suddenly to sniff the air. The fur on her back stood up; her head lowered. Moving like a lioness on the kill, remaining alert, she moved silently forward. The squirrel apparently didn't see her coming. The dog stopped dead still, waited. One paw, then the next, she slowly moved again, ever so close.

"Watch them," whispered the teacher to the students. "Learn from them; they are your teachers now."

Foot by foot, the ground between the squirrel and dog diminished. The squirrel still had its back to the oncoming dog. The dog's eyes were intensely focused on the seemingly unsuspecting squirrel. Without warning, the squirrel dashed away, and the dog leapt forward in a burst of energy. With long, powerful strides, the dog gained on its prey. There were no trees near enough for the squirrel to leap to. Closer and closer, the dog moved in for the kill. This was not play. This was the real drama of all living creatures being enacted before them. Survival — life and death. And yet there was great beauty in the chase.

The squirrel abruptly cut to the left, just as the dog was upon it, and reversed direction, heading back towards the grove of pine trees across the clearing. The dog's momentum took her beyond that sudden turning point. Her turn was slower than the squirrel's, but she was soon back in the chase. Her fur standing straight up on a ridge down her back, her tail straight out, her ears back, her body bounded across the clearing, lessening by leaps the distance between them. The squirrel dashed madly towards the trees; the dog swiftly closed in. Just as they were about to meet, the squirrel dashed up a tree to safety. The dog barked and barked, circling the tree, with eyes still focused on her elusive prey. The squirrel made chattering noises, flicking its tail, jumping from branch to branch, with the dog's eyes following its escape route.

As the students moved forward, the teacher turned and spoke. "Students, life is what it is, neither good nor bad. There is life and there is death. That is the way of things. The squirrel's survival depends on its speed and cunning. Your survival depends not on how well you can defend yourself physically, as animals need to, but on understanding yourself. When you understand the violence within you, you will understand the violence of the world, for they are one and the same thing."

The teacher and students moved on down the path. The river flowed past them on their right as they silently pondered the lessons of life around them. The dog had caught up to them and had run ahead. She stopped again, this time to roll on her back in the cool, wet grass.

"Look, up in the sky. It is our hawk friend again. See how it flies, so silently, effortlessly. The hawk leaves no mark, no trace of itself in the sky. It moves in the moment, with no past. The human being is constantly leaving his mark, and carrying the burden of the past around with him.

"The human being needs to wake from the dreams of the past. He needs to wake up! To look at the beauty of life, to forget himself, his troubles, his memories and enjoy this lovely

earth. But because he is asleep, he all too often destroys the earth and his fellow man. Do you understand, students, do you understand this simple lesson, or are you also asleep?"

The students nodded their understanding, for on these walks only the teacher could speak. They walked over a bridge. The water flowed beneath them, rippling softly down to a lake below. A chipmunk appeared on a decaying log, sat up and took notice of the oncoming group. Then it quickly scampered away into the undergrowth. The clouds, like great balls of cotton, softly mingled together in the blue sky above.

The hawk called, "Enter here, enter here." The river babbled, "Enter here, enter here." And the flowers beckoned, "Enter here." All of nature called, "Enter here." This is the real miracle. "Enter here." The power of the day overwhelmed the smallness of the mind, and the ordinary became extraordinary.

"Dear students, we teachers care for you," the teacher said as they stopped to cool themselves in the shade of the pine trees near the river. "The world is often a dangerous place. This is the challenge you must face. Here we have the opportunity to help you learn about yourself and the world. The true Martial Artist is a person of peace, not a warrior who defends and fights. The real Martial Artist is one who can live gently, caringly, simply in this world. We have been conditioned to think that we should be warriors — ninjas, samurai, cowboys, Indians, or soldiers — on the fields of battle. These are childhood fantasies. But all too often these dreams are acted out by adults, foolishly, in destructive ways.

"Oh, students, can you hear what your teacher is saying? Are you able to hear the simple truths about living a good and kind life? Or are you too filled up with dreams of conquest?

Life, as it is, without illusions and false conquests, is the real challenge. To live as a nobody is the greatest skill, for it is so easy to fill oneself up with the many self-centered dreams that false prophets offer you... at a price. The price is your life, your ability to live in the wonder and beauty of the here and now. Do you understand, dear students? For to live as a nobody, empty, in that there is love."

They sat silently for a long while, the words from the teacher lingering gently in their minds. Honeybees moved from flower to flower, embraced by the bright flame of color each one offered. A hummingbird, wings whirling over one hundred beats a second, whizzed by them, stopping midair in a winged blur. Its body and long narrow beak, however, were perfectly still, poised above a flower. The mind was quiet. *Enter here, enter here.*

An old pine tree preaches wisdom
And a wild bird is crying out truth.

— Old Saying

Chopping Wood, Carrying Water

It was a dark black moonless night. The stars — millions of them — shone brilliant in the cloudless sky. A sky filled with twinkling diamonds, so far away as to stagger the imagination. So far and large were they that the brain could not fully comprehend this glorious mystery. The universe was magnificent!

The fire flickered and danced, sending showers of sparks upwards when a new log was put on. The students had gathered to share their feelings about the essence of their Martial Arts training — not in forms, but in poems and special words selected to evoke similar feelings in the listeners. All were silent in preparation for what might happen — the mystery of life, for a brief moment, fleetingly shared.

A young girl spoke first...

"Dear friends
Life is not a problem to be solved
But a mystery to be enjoyed"

Then silence again. Shadows of thoughtful faces danced in the flickering firelight. Everything else was still.

Another voice, a young man...

"In the forest dark
A pine cone drops
The sound of the water"

Like sparks rising out of the fire and traveling upward to blend with the dark night, these words arose for all to hear, then — like the sparks — they disappeared back from whence they came, into nothingness.

"Oh, look children
An eagle above!
The deer sleep in the forest"

"The kite flying high
The string breaks
That night a full moon"

"The peach blossom blooms
The fruit is not far behind
The children play in the sun"

One after another, the students shared feelings that had been locked away in their hearts just moments before. As each was spoken, it was like a message to the heavens. Each poem seemed to make the stars shine even brighter.

Again there was silence. The fire had slowly burned down to pulsating hot coals. The heat was intensely concentrated in that pile of glowing embers.

The teacher spoke...

"Chopping wood, carrying water,
Oh what a miracle!
The fields lie fallow,
The dark earth awaits the seeds.
Like the empty sky there are no boundaries.
Everything is right in its place, so simple and open.

When you seek to know it, you cannot have it.
You can never capture it,
But you can never lose it.
In not being able to have it, you have it.
When you are silent, it speaks;
When you speak, it is silent.
It is too clear and so it is hard to see.
What you want is always before you,
For it is the moment itself —
There is nowhere to go and nothing to do.
The northern snows are soon to come."

The night was over and everyone went to bed to
dreamless sleep.

Simply trust:
Do not the petals flutter down
Just like that?

— Basho

Mind Like Moon

This was the event the students were all waiting for. No one dared talk about it, but everyone knew that each desired the same thing. Excitement mounted as the day slowly crept on towards the event that would completely transform their concept of what the Martial Arts are about.

The daily chores were finished quickly, the students hurrying around the school, a look of anticipation gleaming in their bright eyes as they passed each other on the way to various tasks. There was no forms practice this day. No usual teacher-student talk either. Just ordinary chores. Everything in the school had to be cleaned thoroughly. Every dusty corner and hidden nook was to be inspected. Even the dog got her bath. The cats hid away, perhaps fearful that they too would be scrubbed and polished like the walls and furniture. The assistant instructors inspected the students' work. With keen eye, they would spot a smudge here, a smear there.

"Cleanliness is attention. It is order. If you want order in your life, start with your dresser drawer," instructed one of the assistants.

The students did not mind these chores. At the beginning they groaned and moaned about cleaning and keeping their rooms tidy, but now they enjoyed the beauty of the order and cleanliness. At one of their very first classes, the teacher said, "Students, bring your shoes here and put them in a pile in front of me." The students ran to get their shoes that were jumbled up in a mess by the practice hall door. They brought them inside and tossed them carelessly into an unsorted, haphazard pile in front of the teacher.

"Now close your eyes," the teacher said to the students.

While their eyes were shut, the teacher mixed the shoes up even more, so that no two were together in the pile.

"Now, open your eyes. Each of you find your shoes quickly!" the teacher commanded.

The students jumped forward and scrambled around the messy pile, bumping into each other, trying to find his or her shoes. Since many looked alike, it was hard to match them up.

"Quickly, quickly, students, find your shoes!"

Finally after what seemed a long while, the students, sweating and frustrated, had their shoes in front of them.

"Now students, wasn't that fun? How easy and simple that was! Yes? No?" the teacher teased.

"No, teacher," the students said in unison.

"Now you understand why we ask our students to put their shoes by the entrance of our place of practice, lining them up just so, taking care to observe the order in this simple gesture. You think that the Art of *Kara-te* is punching and kicking. We know that the Art of *Kara-te* is lining up your shoes — just so. Do you understand?"

"Now take your shoes and line them up with attention, with care — just so — by the door."

The students did as they were asked.

"Now come back. Sit down. And look back at what you've just done. What does it look like to you? How does it make you feel now looking at your shoes?"

"I feel less confused inside, teacher," one of the students responded thoughtfully.

"The shoes look orderly and that makes me feel good," said another.

"Yes," said the teacher. "You have learned another simple yet important lesson in Empty Self."

Now, shoes were lined up — just so — outside the main training hall. The students filed in and sat down with their legs under them in preparation for formal bowing. In the middle of the training hall, there was a large square area, blocked off with red borders. Inside this area, there was a plain wood floor, polished clean and bare by years of careful attention.

A bell sounded and the students sat up straight. Their two chief instructors came in from opposite sides of the room, walking slowly to the center, to that red bordered area. Students moved aside. The chief instructors entered the area and knelt down, facing their students. A bell sounded again and they all bowed to each other — student to teacher — teacher to student — one movement in unison.

The senior assistant instructor arose. "Students, this evening you will be given the opportunity to see your chief instructors in combat."

The air became electric with excitement. The students held their breaths. *Combat! Our chief instructors! But can they fight each other? Isn't that against everything we have been taught?* wondered the bewildered students.

"And this fight will be to the death!" the instructor added.

"What? No! Death?!" the students blurted out. There was confusion, disbelief, fear — and quite a commotion in that training hall.

"Dear students, you read too many ninja tales! No one is going to be hurt. Death in this context is death of the self, not the body. Do you, by now, know the difference? Death is the emptying of that which you are — all the memories, hurts, fears, confusion — the violence of the 'me,' the 'self.' There is nothing to fear! Yet your chief instructors are absolutely serious. This is mortal combat! It is not a demonstration. It is for real! This is life and death, the greatest challenge of all, the ultimate test of one's skill in action."

The students quieted down on hearing these words. *Death of the self?* they thought. *How do you die to yourself in combat?* They had been told over and over again about Empty Self. It had been shown to them in many ways, mostly by observing nature. They remembered the time the school cat caught a mouse and was cruelly playing with it — in a slow death dance. They had tried to stop it, and felt that nature was cruel. But they realized that this was just the way of things. There is life and death. One cannot be separated from the other. Without facing the reality of death, they could not really live fully. They had to empty themselves of all thoughts of right and wrong, good and evil, and let their natural response to life run through them. They had learned that spontaneous natural action brings about real feelings, real emotions and right action. But they had never been shown Empty Self in serious human combat.

The students became very quiet as the two chief instructors turned towards each other. *Won't the man overpower the woman? Isn't he stronger than she is? Even though they are both chief instructors, doesn't the male have the advantage over the female?* they thought. This had been a secret debate among the students for a long while. Now they were going to find out.

Slowly the chief instructors rose, staring intently at each other. Everyone in the room was focused on them. The instructors bowed slowly and with great dignity to each other. Both were wearing their formal outfits — white *gi* tops and black *hakama* skirts. They both took their fighting stances. Like colossal mountains, they faced each other.

For what seemed like years, these two chief instructors faced each other! There was not a flicker of inattention, not a moment's lack of awareness; their eyes were locked, as if they were one. It was incredible, and yet so natural, like when the dog spotted the squirrel just before the chase began.

Then, ever so slowly, at a snail's pace, the two circled each other, never at any time letting down their guard. This was the lesson of the unbroken flame of attention. This absolute intensity left no room for the past and its distractions. Even the tiniest lapse of attention was not possible. It was as if they were one whole, undivided movement, working together to create an incredible yet simple event. There was nothing magical about what was happening, yet there was a beauty, a magic that occurs naturally and simply in nature.

There were no spectacular displays of superhuman power. No boards, bricks, blocks of ice, stones or bones being broken by gnarled and hardened hands. No incredible flying kicks through the air, as if off spring boards. No frightening sound effects to excite the mind into a frenzy of blood lust. There was only a quiet yet deafening attention, a relationship of sensitivity and cooperation. This was true Mastership!

After what seemed like a long, long while, the two chief instructors — without ever offensively striking out at each other — lowered their guard and resumed the ready stance.

Kneeling down, they bowed to each other, touching their foreheads to the bare worn wooden floor. It was over! And yet — it had just begun!

The old pond
A frog jumps in
Plop!

— Basho

The Riddle's Answer

The students had come together after another stormy night. Tree branches had fallen, broken off in a fierce wind. A few clouds still drifted in the morning sky. The ground was soaked by the downpour. The air was clean and fresh, the sun breaking through to warm the earth.

Last night, just before the storm came, they practiced their forms in the main hall. Ceremoniously they had lit dozens of candles to illuminate their practice area. In the flickering of those yellow lights, they moved with grace and ease, playing with their shadows on the wall.

The room today was clean and dry. The smell of burnt wood, sweat, and candle wax filled the air with a strange pungent sweet odor. The students rose and bowed as the chief instructors entered. Then they all sat quietly for a while, letting their minds relax.

Then one of the teachers spoke: "Why is there so much sorrow in the world? Why do people fight and kill each other? How can you, as a Martial Artist, live peacefully through your Art? Have you ever seriously thought about these questions? Or are you caught up in fanciful images of attack and defense?" The students were quiet and listened intently.

"When you leave here and go back to your regular lives, what will you take home from here? What difference will all of this training mean to your lives? Have you understood what we are teaching?"

A bird sang outside the window. The cats on the window ledge stretched, yawned, then went back to sleep.

"Oh students, the world is a maze and you have to find your way through it without getting lost. It is so easy to get lost. There are so many false signposts, so many dead ends that you can get caught up in — even for a lifetime. This is no childhood game. You are growing up and need to become strong and capable. It is our job as teachers to help you understand yourself and the world, to give you skills — not just to read and write, but to live in relationship peacefully. This is the real meaning of your education here. We hope that you have some sense of this. I know that your stay here has sometimes been hard. You probably haven't completely understood what we are trying to demonstrate. But no matter, don't worry. Just listen and someday it will all make sense. Just keep your minds open, like a newly plowed field. If your field is fertile, the seeds will grow."

The students were so very still. They knew that what was being said was of great importance to their lives, and that the teachers cared deeply for them. The students had come to this place with all kinds of romantic ideas about the Martial Arts, with spectacular desires to be great warriors, like the ninjas or samurais of old. But they had grown up a lot here and were filled with a new wisdom. They knew the true and right meaning of *Kara-te*, the Art of the Martial Arts.

"Oh, students, be beginners!" the teacher called out. "What meaning does the past have for you? Can you remember a time of anger, of sorrow, of fear? Why? Live *now*, students! Let the old run through you like a river. Just listen, observe, then let it go. Memories are with you but they should not interfere with your living in the present. All those images you have are just that: images. They cannot harm you. They have no place in living. Living is always new, fresh. Your memories are old, stale, dead. To understand this is true meditation. Meditation is not repeating something over and over. That only dulls the mind, puts it to sleep. Meditation means to be aware, to look at, to see. And you can do it anytime, wherever you are. Just stop — look — and listen! When old fears creep back into your brain, just say, 'hello — goodbye!' And have a beginner's mind."

The students felt warm inside, as they did when they first put their shoes in order by the training hall door — just so. They felt healthy and happy, and most of all, cared for. Realizing that their special training time together for this session was coming to a close, they also felt sad.

"It's all right to cry when one feels sad. This is as natural as cherry blossoms falling from a tree in spring," their teacher said with tears in her eyes. Both of the teachers cried in silence with their students. The sun came out fully from behind the clouds and warm rays flooded the training hall.

"One last thing, dear students. What is it that you cannot see, cannot hear, cannot take hold of, is silent when you speak, speaks when you are silent, and you can only have when you don't want it? Answer, and you will not know; don't answer and you will be a fool!"

With these words the teachers looked at each one of the students.

"Can you now tell me the meaning of Empty Self?"

The two elected senior students stood, walked up to the teachers, and held out their hands to them. In the students' hands were dandelion flowers: lovely, common, beautifully brilliant yellow weeds.

The teachers accepted the flowers, stood up, bowed, and left the training hall. The formal class was over, but the training would remain with the students throughout their lives.

To be continued –

*Be patient with all
that is unresolved in your heart
and learn to love the questions
themselves.*

— Rainer Maria Rilke

To the Young Reader

Welcome, students! You have just finished the first book in the series, "Tales of the Empty-Handed Masters." My name is Sensei (teacher) Terrence Webster-Doyle; I have studied and taught the Martial Arts for over 30 years. The basic intention of this series is to portray the Martial Arts as a universal endeavor that will help you to understand and resolve conflict peacefully — both individually and globally.

The essence of all Martial Arts is "Empty Self," a term that comes from the word *Kara-te*. Empty Self is that state where one is free of self-centered thinking and action, that is, selfishness — which has its roots in fear and the instinct for self-survival. Self-centeredness, being separated from other human beings — individually or collectively — creates tremendous conflict in the world. It is this self-centeredness or selfishness that is at the root of our conflict; understanding this self-centeredness is the focus of Martial Arts practice.

The term *Kara-te* first meant "Chinese Hands." It later became known as "Empty Hands" — a weaponless form of combat. This form of self-defense used blocking, punching, kicking, and striking as a way to protect oneself from attack. The physical self-defense form called "Karate" developed over time into the various styles of combat training taught in China, Korea, Okinawa, and Japan today.

In the early part of the 19th century, a Karate teacher named Gichin Funakoshi saw that Karate was more than just a physical form of self-defense. He saw that the practice of Karate gave one an insight into conflict and could provide the foundation for an intelligent and peaceful way of life. It was at this time that the term *Kara-te* changed in meaning from "Empty Hands" to "Empty Self."

I use the term *Kara-te* as it applies not only to Karate itself but to all Martial Art forms. Every style of self-defense has *Kara-te* (Empty Self) at its center. Whether your style or particular Martial Art is Chinese, Korean, Japanese, or Okinawan, the basic intent should be to discover Empty Self and the end to conflict. The serious Martial Art student will discover that, indeed, the root of conflict is within us, originating in self-centeredness and fear.

Some people ask, "How can the Martial Arts bring about peace? Aren't the Martial Arts concerned with violence?" Let's look at that for a moment. If you want to learn about ecology, for example, you might examine pollution, its effects, and how it originates. You would look at the actuality of pollution to see what creates it. Similarly, if you want to learn about violence and what causes it, you need to be able to look at it closely. This doesn't mean that you must travel to a battle zone! However, you would look for a real source to study, to discover how violence originates — and the Martial Arts provide an excellent way to examine this directly.

The Martial Arts can do great harm when used in actual combat — but they can also be used to bring about peace by helping people to understand what creates conflict, violence, and war. The fundamental insight in understanding the root of war is understanding what Empty Self means — not intellectually, as in remembering a science formula, but by really living it.

I have written this book to share with you the great importance of the Art of *Kara-te*, of all Martial Arts, in understanding conflict and ending war, both within ourselves and in the world. I hope that as you read this book, you questioned all that was written — for only in questioning do you find out for yourself. You are your own Master, for within you is the ability to know truth — and the understanding necessary to end violence, conflict, and war.

Empty Self is the foundation of all Martial Arts,
and at the heart of Empty Self is peace.

To the Adult Reader

I have offered the preceding tales, some traditional and some drawn from my own experiences, as a way for young people to begin to understand the essence of all Martial Arts — that is, "Empty Self" — freedom from conflict and the violence conflict produces. All these tales are true, in the sense that they are of real value. Too often Martial Arts practice is primarily concerned with self-defense skills. These skills are important in that they help students gain the confidence needed to avoid the usual automatic, biologically conditioned "fight or flight" reaction. Having this confidence, students can learn — through role playing, for example — how to get out of a potentially harmful situation by using creative, peaceful means. When fear is reduced, the student has the presence of mind to use the host of nonviolent alternatives that he or she has practiced to quell the fear and aggression in another.

But beyond this, the "Art of Empty Self" is a means by which students can learn to observe their minds and the conditioned views that they, and all of us, have — views that create conflict in relationship between individuals and in the world at large. Helping young people understand themselves by using a Martial Art is providing them with a sensible, fun, and practical way to learn about the nature and structure of conflict. As Martial Artists, educators, parents, school administrators, and counselors, we have the unique opportunity of creating an environment for young people that can assist them in creating healthy and intelligent relationships. Many people think that studying a Martial Art will only increase the expression of violence by the young person. This may be true if instruction is limited to physical self-defense. But if the young person is exposed to the totality of what a Martial Art offers, both physical *and* mental training, then he or she will be better able to understand and creatively cope with aggression. The essence of Martial Arts training is to observe and be free of conflict, not to create more.

In my own classes, I encourage students to exercise their brains — the most powerful "muscle" they have. For rank advancement, they are required not only to demonstrate their physical self-defense forms, but also their understanding of "Empty Self"— its relationship to their daily lives and to personal and global well-being. As a Martial Artist, educator, parent, former school administrator, and counselor, I have found that young people need proper guidance in understanding themselves in relationship. We, as adults, too often neglect this aspect of their lives, focusing intensively on academic and intellectual prowess. Academic subjects, of course, have an important place in education, but without equal emphasis on understanding relationship, education is out of balance. If taught rightly, the Martial Arts can be an excellent way for young people to achieve a balance — through the (*seemingly* contradictory) peaceful practice of the "Art of Empty Self."

ABOUT THE AUTHOR

Dr. Terrence Webster-Doyle, Founder and Chief Instructor of Take Nami Do Karate and the Director of the Shuhari Institute — A Center for the Study of the Martial Arts, has studied and taught Karate for over 30 years, has a doctorate degree in psychology, and is a credentialed secondary and community college instructor. He earned his Black Belt in the Japanese style of Gensei Ryu Karate from Sensei Numano in 1967. He has worked in Juvenile Delinquency Prevention, taught at the university level in education, psychology and philosophy, and developed counseling programs for young people. Dr. Webster-Doyle is currently the Director of the Atrium Society. He and his wife Jean are co-parenting five daughters.

Dr. Terrence Webster-Doyle and Rod Cameron can be contacted through the Atrium Society (see address and phone number on facing page).

ABOUT THE ARTIST

Rod Cameron was born in 1948 in Chicago, Illinois, but has lived in Southern California most of his life. He studied painting with the renowned illustrator, Keith Ward, and at the Otis/Parsons School of Design in Los Angeles, California.

Rod has been designing and illustrating for over 20 years; his work has been shown on major network television and has received 17 awards for illustrative excellence.

114

ABOUT THE PUBLISHER

Atrium Society concerns itself with fundamental issues which prevent understanding and cooperation in human affairs. Starting with the fact that our minds are conditioned by our origin of birth, our education and our experiences, the intent of the Atrium Society is to bring this issue of conditioning to the forefront of our awareness. Observation of the fact of conditioning — becoming directly aware of the movement of thought and action — brings us face-to-face with the actuality of ourselves. Seeing who we actually are, not merely what we think we are, reveals the potential for a transformation of our ways of being and relating.

If you would like more information, please write or call us. We enjoy hearing from people who read our books and we appreciate your comments.

Atrium Society
P.O. Box 816
Middlebury, Vermont 05753
Tel: (802) 388-0922
Fax: (802) 388-1027
For book order information:
(800) 848-6021

ABOUT THE SHUHARI INSTITUTE

The intention of the Shuhari Institute is to bring together the people and resources that give an intelligent perspective to the Martial Arts, and to disseminate thought provoking and insightful information about its creative aspects through literature, videotapes, classes, workshops and conferences. Dr. Webster-Doyle conducts workshops in New England, and in other areas upon request. For more information, contact the Atrium Society (see address and phone number above).

BOOKS by Dr. TERRENCE WEBSTER-DOYLE

For Adults —

Karate:
The Art of Empty Self
One Encounter, One Chance:
The Essence of the Art of Karate

THE "SANE AND INTELLIGENT LIVING" SERIES
Growing Up Sane:
Understanding the Conditioned Mind
Brave New Child:
Education for the 21st Century
The Religious Impulse:
A Quest for Innocence
Peace — The Enemy of Freedom:
The Myth of Nonviolence

For Young People —

THE "EDUCATION FOR PEACE" SERIES (AGES 7-15)
Facing the Double-Edged Sword:
The Art of Karate for Young People
Tug of War:
Peace Through Understanding Conflict
Fighting the Invisible Enemy:
Understanding the Effects of Conditioning
Why is Everybody Always Picking on Me?:
A Guide to Handling Bullies

THE "MARTIAL ARTS FOR PEACE" SERIES (AGES 10-17)
Eye of the Hurricane:
Tales of the Empty-Handed Masters
Maze of the Fire Dragon:
Tales of the Empty-Handed Masters
Flight of the Golden Eagle:
Tales of the Empty-Handed Masters

HOW TO USE THESE BOOKS
IN A MARTIAL ARTS PROGRAM

Dr. Webster-Doyle's books can add quality and spirit to Martial Arts programs and are available at bulk discounts to Martial Arts schools and organizations. The books have been widely used:

- As part of the introductory membership package for new students
- As required reading for rank advancement
- As awards for performance or improvement
- As books for sale in the school's store
- As available reading in the school library
- As material to read aloud and discuss during class

ORDERING INFORMATION

To learn more about Atrium Society Publications' special discounts for Martial Arts programs, to place orders, or to request a free catalog, please write or call:

Atrium Society Publications / Shuhari Institute
P.O. Box 816
Middlebury, Vermont 05753
Toll Free: 1-800-848-6021

Dr. Webster-Doyle is available for workshops in your area.
Please contact us at the above address.